H.C Beeching

Love in Idleness

A Volume of Poems

H.C Beeching

Love in Idleness
A Volume of Poems

ISBN/EAN: 9783744717243

Printed in Europe, USA, Canada, Australia, Japan

Cover: Foto ©Thomas Meinert / pixelio.de

More available books at **www.hansebooks.com**

LOVE IN IDLENESS

A VOLUME OF POEMS

LONDON
KEGAN PAUL, TRENCH & CO., 1, PATERNOSTER SQUARE
1883

To Andrew Cecil Bradley

CONTENTS

LOVE IN IDLENESS

	PAGE
To Erato	3
In Scheria	5
Amoret	19
The Recompense	21
Song, "Is this the Spring?"	23
May-Day	24
In Limine	27
A Song of the Three Kings	30
A Roseleaf	32
Song, "Love walked upon the Sea"	33
Afternoon	34
Ballade	39
To Comatas	41
Rondeau	43
"Rose and Lily"	44
Nocturne—Chopin, op. 40, 2	45
„ „ 37, 1	46
Loca Senta Sitv	49
A Pastoral	51
Lvna Fatifera	53
Opisthen	55
Vigilate Itaqve	57

	PAGE
Song of Hylas	59
Secvndvm Altitvdinem Caeli a Terra	62
The History of Philip the Deacon	65
On a Drawing of Lionardo in the Academy at Venice	75
Lines by a Person of Quality	77
Concerning Acme and Septimius (from Catullus)	78
For a Drawing	80
From the Italian of Giovanni dell' Isola	82
Magdalen Walks in Winter	84
Separation	85
Litany	86
Tyrus	89
Artifex ad Artem	92
Santa Cruz	94

DOGGEREL IN DELFT

Life and Death	103
Chimes	104
Half-way in Love	106
Tricolor	109
To M. A. C. G.	110
Monologue d'Outre Tombe	112
To the Nightingale in September	116
The Last Tennis-Party	118
Ballade of Dead Thinkers	122
Some Flowers	124
Rondel	126
Triolet	127

CONTENTS ix

SONNETS

	PAGE
THE LOST SELF	131
PVLVIS ET VMBRA	132
UNDER THE CANOPY	133
ITALIAM NON SPONTE SEQVOR	134
LOVE UNRETURNED	135
THINGS NEW AND OLD (two sonnets) ...	136
JEALOUSY	138
MADONNA INCOGNITA ...	139
THE EMPTY PLACE	140
BEFORE PARTING ...	141
AFTER PARTING	142
MAGDALEN GARDENS AND MAGDALEN BRIDGE (two sonnets)	143
SUMMER AND WINTER	145
IRELAND, 1881	146
,, 1882	147
ON THE BIRTH OF VENUS BY BOTTICELLI	148
ON A DRAWING BY BURNE JONES	149
VENVS MATVTINA	150
THE HANDMAID OF THE LORD	151
ON A MADONNA AND CHILD BY BELLINI ...	152
THE NATURE OF THINGS	153

TRANSLATIONS FROM THE GREEK

		PAGE
From Meleager I. χείματος ἠνεμόεντος	... ...	157
II. πλέξω λευκόϊον	... ...	159
III. ἤδη λευκόϊον θάλλει	... ...	160
IV. οὐ γάμον ἀλλ' Ἀΐδαν	...	161
V. ἠοῦς ἄγγελε, χαῖρε	...	162
VI. ἔγχει καὶ πάλιν εἰπέ		163
VII. δάκρυά σοι καὶ νέρθε	... ...	164
VIII. κηρύσσω τὸν ἔρωτα ...	...	165
IX. ζωροπότει δύσερως	... ...	166
X. ἁδὺ μέλος ναὶ Πᾶνα ...	...	167
From Sappho, κατθάνοισα δὲ κείσεαι ...	... ..	168
From Alcman, οὔ μ'ἔτι παρθενικαί	... ...	169
From Callimachus, ὤφελε μηδ' ἐγένοντο	... ...	170
From Menander, Hypobolimæus frag. 2	.. ...	171
From Leonidas, ὁ πλόος ὡραῖος	... ...	172
From Theocritus, I. ἄνθρωπε ζωῆς περιφείδεο	...	173
II. Δάφνις ὁ λευκόχρως	... ...	174
A Vintage Song (from Agathias), ἡμεῖς μὲν πατέοντες		175
The Swallow Song, ἦλθ' ἦλθε χελιδών	... ...	177
From Sophocles, I. Frag. 713, Dind. ...	...	179
II. ,, 162 ,,	... ...	180
From the Iliad, Bk. iv. ll. 422-456	... ...	181

LOVE IN IDLENESS

TO ERATO

Love is a rose, say some; in May
    It buds, by genial winds caressed;
Tender to touch, but wellaway
    Its thorns run deep if idly prest;
    It may be; yet it may be guessed
Flowers grow as sweet, and weaponless,
    All the long year from East to West:
Our love is love-in-idleness.

Love is a toil, say some; and they
    Labour to love by love oppressed,
And weary night brings weary day
    If so be they may get them blest;
    Yea, of all toil the weariest
Is that wherewith they strive to bless
    Their aching heart and longing breast:
Our love is love in idleness.

TO ERATO

Love is a god, say some; alway
   A jealous god most manifest,
More swift to hear than we to pray,
   Mid mortals an unbidden guest;
   Yet hath he given a day of rest,
Whereon we worship none the less
   For that we toil not, neither jest:
Our Love is Love in idleness.

Envoy.

Princess, this love is even our best;
   Take it, Love's sovereign votaress,
To whom our vows are now addressed:
   Our love is love in idleness.

IN SCHERIA

PART I.

"When the star was brightest aloft that goes ever heralding the dawning of the daylight, then the sea-travelling ship drew nigh to the island."—*Odyssey*, b. xiii. ll. 93–5.

By this they have the island well in sight,
Its faint fields gleaming through the mist; all night
  Have they swept on, the dark waves off the stem
Gurgling; and now the morning star is bright.

Only four days ago with cart and mules
We drove to where the running water cools
  The round white pebbles, slipping over them,
In the bright meadow-bordered river pools.

There came he on us from the forest dim,
Sea worn, but like a god in face and limb;
  Even a king's daughter, wonderful and fair,
Might lose her heart unblamed to one like him.

IN SCHERIA

O splendour of the sunset as we went
Past the ploughed fields to where the poplars bent
   About Athene's spring that, rising there,
Down the King's Meadow its white water sent!

And there I left him, and drove down apace
Between the shipyards, through the market-place,
   While all the air seem'd sweet and musical,
For next day I should see him face to face,

And the day after, and for ever thus:
For he would stay here and be one of us,
   Dwelling at ease within our palace hall
Clad in soft raiment, great and glorious.

Ah me, the ways untrod, the words unsaid!
The tender memories unremembered!
   The dreadful presence of what might have been,
And life eternal of things done and dead!

One word of parting was to serve for all,
One last short word, when to the festival
   He came at evening, his face flushed and keen
With thoughts of home; and high along the hall

The great gold statues held their torches red.
I spoke, with loud seas swirling in my head,
   Farewell: remember that to me this day
Thou owest thy life's ransom. Then he said

Some words in answer: his voice sounded dim,
Far off: the silver pillars seemed to swim
   Before me; and he spoke and passed away,
And that was the last word I had of him.

All the next day they sat along the hall
And feasted till the sun began to fall,
   And the last healths were drunk; then silently
The oarsmen, and he far above them all,

Went shorewards, where the swift ship rocking lay;
And the sun sank, and all the paths were grey;
   Then bent they to the oars, and murmuringly
The purple water cleft and gave them way.

The twisting-horned slow-swinging oxen low.
Across the fields: light waves in even flow
   Plash on the beach: but when he went from us
The morning and the sunlight seemed to go.

The gods are angry: we shall never be
Now as of old, when far from all men we
    Dwelt in a lonely land and languorous,
Circled and sundered by the sleeping sea.

Yea, the Olympians then were wont to go
Among us, visible godheads, to and fro;
    So far we lived from any sight or touch
Of evil, in the sea's engirdling flow.

What now if Lord Poseidon, as men say,
Be wroth against us, and will choke the bay
    With a great mountain?—yet I care not much:
All things are grown the same since yesterday.

Why should I live where everything goes wrong,
Where hope is dead and only grief lasts long?
    I will have rest among the asphodel;
For death is stronger, though my love be strong.

There will I see the women he did see,
Leda and Tyro and Antiope
    And Ariadne, queens that loved too well
Of old, and ask them if they loved like me.

The last white stars grow fainter one by one;
The folding mists rise up to meet the sun;
   Birds twitter on our dewy orchard trees;
Day comes: alas, my day is nearly done.

(He is on land in Ithaca by this.)
Come now, I pray thee, and with one soft kiss
   Draw the life out of me and give me ease,
Queen golden-shafted, maiden Artemis.

Part II.

"The sailing of Cinyras, which he told to Lucianus and his fellows, being released out of prison in the Five Islands, and joining them thereafter in the City of Lamps."—*Vera Historia*, b. iii. ch. 7.

Thence we sailed forward for a night and day,
Across blue breadths of water, touched with spray
   Beneath a south-west wind, that steadily
Sped us along our undiscovered way.

But when, gold clouds about him for attire,
The low broad sun, a lamp of crimson fire,
   Sank in the west, we looked across the sea,
And saw far off the land of our desire.

One mountain peak where sky and water ceased,
Rising against the flush that girt the east,
  Snow-crowned, steep-falling, while our ship ran on,
Above the purple waste of waves increased.

And the sun sank, and all the sea was grey
Before us ; and behind us, where the day
  Lingered north-westward, still the water shone
Opaline, where the keel had cloven its way.

So we sailed forward through the falling night
In the night wind, while ever on our right
  Orion wheeled his slowly blazing belt,
And two large planets rose and sank from sight

Low in the south : and now the stars outspread
Drew westward, and the summer dew was shed
  Wet on the deck and cordage, and we felt
Rather than saw the island, straight ahead,

A vast low shadow in the glimmering sea ;
Whereon the breaking rollers ceaselessly
  Moaned through the darkness as they struck the sand
On that untrodden shore where we would be.

IN SCHERIA

At last we saw their white foam faintly shine
Around our feet, and on the extreme sea line
   We beached the ship, and leapt ourselves on land,
And sleeping waited for the morn divine.

But when the rosy fingered morn on high,
The lady of the light, had climbed the sky,
   We rose and sought about us, where the way
Up to the city of our search might lie.

A mile of river meadow, where the grass
Knee-deep and dewy swayed to let us pass,
   We crossed, while through the morning misty-grey
Shot gleams of colour as from shining brass.

The air was still around us; only nigh
Upon our left the river murmured by;
   And far behind the lapping waves at play
Washed on the shingle undistinguishably.

Then the path turned and left the meadow land,
Winding through cornfields high on either hand,
   Till on the ridge we climbed, where nigh the way
About a fountain many poplars stand.

And now we faced the morning; and the brown
Heads of the ripe wheat were bowed softly down
    And the mist broken in the morning breeze :
And looking forward we could see the town.

A road and double row of shipyards ran
Between two bays to where the walls began,
    With a white temple and palace girt with trees
Beyond, but nowhere any sign of man.

Then we descended towards it, and on all
A silence came; we did not speak or call;
    And our dark-eyed sweet-voicèd passenger
Led on, until we came below the wall.

But as we entered—how can mortal tell
In mortal words the marvel that befel?
    Whether you will believe I hardly care;
I know I should have disbelieved as well—

Suddenly out of nothing seemed to spring
All round us, clasping us as in a ring,
    Whence risen or how passed through is marvellous,
A mountain, vast and overshadowing.

IN SCHERIA

Sheer-sided it engirt us, towering high
All round, but open far above, whereby
   Some little light fell down and came to us ;
So that we saw the stars within the sky,

The seven stars sickle-wise above our head.
And we walked dumbly on, astonished,
   Unwitting what we did or whence we came,
Following where the twilit pathway led.

At last a gleam of firelight led us on
To where afar the palace doorway shone,
   Lit as for banquet; but the flickering flame
Fell on bare places whence the guests were gone.

Faintly the scent of burning cedar rolled
About the tapestries that fold on fold
   Drooped on the walls : in double line thereby
Stood torches held by torch-bearers of gold.

There, on a couch with spices overstrewn,
And coverings coruscant with precious stone,
   Clad in a robe of strange Sidonian dye
Sea-coloured, lay a sleeping girl alone.

Breathless we stood, and did not dare to stir,
Fearing some wizardry still deadlier;
   But he who led us half restrained a cry,
And went straight forward and stooped down to her.

Lo, when a soft rain from the warm wet south
Lights on the grass that pants at noon for drouth,
   Even so, so softly and so tenderly,
He bent above her and kissed her on the mouth.

And in that moment's space from shore and bay
The mountain without hands was rolled away,
   And all around us freer and splendider
Than ever elsewhere poured the golden day.

But through the girl a quiver limb by limb
Ran, and her dark eyes opened and grew dim,
   As without any word he grew to her,
Trembling all over; and she grew to him.

And when I turned my eyes away from this,
Giddy with sight of their new lover's bliss,
   My eyes upon the shining land came down
That seemed no longer strange: I could not miss

That mountain outline and that curve of shore,
That harbour with the swingingships that bore
　　No rudder on their crooked sterns: the town
And people seemed as things long known before.

As thus I wondered, like a sound long spent
In dreams re-echoed, through my lips there went
　　The old surging rhythm of "these Phæacian men
Who dwelt of old time nigh the violent

Tribe of the Cyclops, in the lawns outspread
Of Hypereia, and were sore bestead
　　For lack of might before their raids: so then
Divine Nausithoüs raised them up and led

And set in Scheria, far from men that win
Wealth by their trade, and walled the city in,
　　And builded houses and made temples fair,
And gave them share and share of tilth therein;

But he ere now was gone, struck down of fate,
To darkness, and Alcinoüs held his state,
　　Skilled in wise counsel of the gods; and there
Grey-eyed Athene lighted at his gate."

This was the land that many men desire,
In other lands where other pleasures tire.
   Yet one alone might there find resting-place,
Having attained through many a flood and fire;

Even he who sailed with us across the wan
Reaches of tossing water.   Not a man
   But named him now by name, and in his face
Gazed long, and knew him for the Ithacan.

For us, our resting was not won as yet,
For other shores our windy sails were set;
   Ah, and we might not sojourn in the place
Where they who sojourn all their pain forget.

So but short time we lingered: for the wind
Fair streaming eastward blew and brought to mind
   The old companions of our wandering race,
Whose swifter sails had left our crew behind.

And autumn grew, and swallows on the wing
Gathered for flight, and songs that reapers sing
   Were over, and along the field paths went
Girls with piled baskets red for vintaging.

And the time neared of wrecks on sea and sand,
And streaming storms on many a wave-lashed strand
   Without, tho' here no wind were violent,
Nor storm could trouble that enchanted land.

For the last time we feasted there arow
In the king's palace, when the sun grew low,
   Deep into night with all our company;
And in the morning we embarked to go.

The bay lay quiet in the slant sunshine,
The white rocks quivering in it; but, divine,
   Fresh and wind-stirred, far out the open sea
Rolled in a rough green violet-hollowed line.

We entered in and at the thwarts sate down;
And at our going all the Scherian town
   Stood thronged to speed us; softly in the heat
The water rippled through the oar-blades brown.

And through the palace garden he and she,
Hand clasped in hand, came down beside the sea,
   And hailed us one by one with voices sweet,
And bade farewell and all prosperity.

Then our oars dipped together, and the spray
Flashed in a million sparkles round our way,
   As we with rowing swift and strenuous
Shot out across the sleepy sunlit bay.

There on the white sea verge, till all the strand
Grew dim behind us, still I saw them stand
   In the low sunlight: if they looked at us
I know not; but they stood there hand in hand.

AMORET

I.

LOVE found you still a child,
Who looked on him and smiled
Scornful with laughter mild
    And knew him not:
Love turned and looked on you,
Love looked and he smiled too,
And all at once you knew
    You knew not what.

II.

Love laughed again, and said
Smiling, "Be not afraid:
Though lord of all things made,
    I do no wrong:
Like you I love all flowers,
All dusky twilight hours,
Spring sunshine and spring showers,
    Like you am young."

III.

Love looked into your eyes,
Your clear cold idle eyes,
Said, "These shall be my prize,
  Their light my light;
These tender lips that move
With laughter soft as love
Shall tremble still and prove
  Love's very might."

IV.

Love took you by the hand
At eve, and bade you stand
At edge of the woodland,
  Where I should pass;
Love sent me thither, sweet,
And brought me to your feet;
He willed that we should meet,
  And so it was.

THE RECOMPENSE

I CALLED on Love and I said:
I have eaten ashes for bread,
I have mingled my drink with tears
              All these years.

I have watched while others slept,
I have ofttimes fasted and wept,
I have taken no delight
              Day or night.

What hast thou done for me
Who have given my life to thee,
And have paid ceaseless vows
              In thy house?

I have humbled myself at thy feet,
And have taken bitter for sweet,
And have striven to fulfil
              All thy will.

THE RECOMPENSE

Hast thou brought me any nigher
To the end of my desire?
Or what guerdon hast thou given,
    Love in heaven?

I am weak and thou art strong,
And thou hast proved me long;
What hast thou given, O Lord,
    For reward?

I cried upon Love and he heard
And he answered me but a word;
From the height of heaven above
    Love said, Love.

SONG

TO L. S.

Is this the spring that wanders
　With sad and wistful eyes,
And idly inly ponders
　The grey and vacant skies?
Is this true spring or seeming
　That sits with sunken head?
O yes, for she is dreaming
　Of winter that is dead.

Is this the spring that quickens
　The violets in the vale,
And all the woodland thickens
　With primrose-blossoms pale?
Is this true spring or seeming
　That smiles along the way?
O yes, for she is dreaming
　Of laughter of the May.

MAY-DAY

May-Day is gone, we go on different ways,
This is the last of all our old May-days;
But separate or together scarce our feet
Will find another pathway quite so sweet.
Then, since it is the last time, let me sing
As to the music of your listening;
O gold and ivory flower of perfect face
Born in some distant sun-replenished place!
O myrrh and cinnamon whose vapour rolled
Around the seven sacred lamps of gold!

Will you remember, as the days go on,
The trees that budded and the fields that shone,
While overhead the burning afternoon
Glowed as if May had caught the heart of June,
And filled the curving river-spaces lone
With scent of rose and hawthorn yet unblown?
Under strange softness as of southern skies
Spring paused and lingered with reverted eyes,

And in mid pulse and passion of the year
Stayed for a moment's flight, that earth might hear
In all her windy heights and hollow vales
The sweet sad echo of last year's nightingales;
Might hear the undistinguishable sea,
Might feel hot scent of thyme abundantly
On downs where utmost August burned the wheat
And blood-red poppies faint with heavy heat.

So swiftly with the swift-descending day
The river's coils unwound and gave us way;
Where westward lay the level meads unrolled
Yellow for miles with bright marsh-marigold.
And evermore the boat's swift shade outran
The ripple of the wavering water wan;
The banks drew backward and the ripple spread;
The light spray from the oar-blades diamonded
The sleeping water where the lilies grew
Tall golden green among the gold-shot blue.
Thus we sped onward as the sun drew down
And passed the willows and drew near the town.
Deep in the east a single planet pale
Glimmered against the misty purple veil,
When many bells at once began to ring.

And so we parted about lamplighting,
And the sweet day was dead: and from afar
Calm and disconsolate the evening star
Trembled south-westward in a grey-green sky
Where yet the last dim orange lingeringly
Glowed faint and fainter: then the darkness fell
Fold upon fold, till hardly visible
The spires stood out against the starlit night.
The heaven of heavens stood open to the sight
Bared for a space: and softly over all
Low sound went echoing like the plash and fall
Of breaking waves upon a moonlit strand
In some forgotten and forgetful land.

IN LIMINE

Before the House of Love there stand,
With heavy heart and empty hand,
Many and many, saying thus:
O Love our Lord, be piteous!

Lo, these are they of whom we are,
Whose feet have come from very far:
Whom long ago, amid the hum
Of restless hours that go and come,
With light once come and never gone
Love's eyes have turned and looked upon;
And once for their delight and dread,
As here they wandered chance-footed,
Within his courts, beneath his gate
Love's lyre has grown articulate.

Too happy they, if once of all
The many days that fade and fall,
One day to a strange softness grown
His voice has answered to their own;
If once in some green-shadowed place
Their eyes have risen and seen his face,
Too happy! well content with this,
To be for ever where he is.

But we who on his threshold stone
Long days and nights have knelt alone,
Whose lips are tired, whose eyes are dim
With tears and prayers unheard of him,
To whom the Lord of man's delight
Gives fire by day and cloud by night;
What light is left for all our need
From him who is our light indeed?

We strive not, neither cry; we know
Since he hath said it, it is so.
For what are we, that for our sake
The iron links of fate should break,
That for our sake untied should be
The knot of love's fatality?

IN LIMINE

One silent moment, deep in awe,
His awful face unveiled we saw,
And for that last lost moment's sight
Our path is henceforth in the night.
Cold gleaming from the depth divine
Some star may yet arise and shine
With pallid beams to mark our way;
But not the sunlight, not the day.

A SONG OF THE THREE KINGS

"And finding by the sudden waning of the brightest star that the Blessed Virgin was sick, they made haste to take all manner of healing herbs and depart to Nazareth. But when they found her already dead, they returned sorrowfully to their own country."
—*History of the Three Kings.*

SHE is dead, ah, she is dead,
   Silent is that gentle breath,
Still and low that golden head,
   That sweet mouth is stopped in death.
Wherefore now we bring to her
Gold and frankincense and myrrh.

She is dead, yes, she is dead,
   Never may we see again
Purest holiest maidenhead,
   Mother without spot or stain.
Mid the sleeping lilies fold
Myrrh and frankincense and gold.

A SONG OF THE THREE KINGS

    Lo, we come from very far
        With all simples that we have,
    Caspar, Melchior, Balthasar,
        Ah, we came too late to save.
    Scatter we ere we go hence
    Gold and myrrh and frankincense.

A ROSELEAF

O sweetest face of all the faces
    About the way;
A light for night and lonely places,
    A day in day;
If you will touch and take and pardon
    What I can give,
Take this, a flower into your garden,
    And bid it live.
It is not worth your love or praises
    For aught its own;
But Proserpine would smile on daisies
    Sicilian-grown.
And so beneath your smile a minute
    May this rest too;
Although the only virtue in it
    Be love of you.
My flower may droop in rainy weather,
    In drought may pine,
If for its day it link together
    Your name with mine.

SONG

Love walked upon the sea this tranced night, I know,
  For the waves beneath his feet ran pale with silver light,
  But he brought me no message as on a summer night,
A golden summer night, long ago.

Love walked among the fields of yellow waving corn,
  For the poppy blossomed red where his weary feet had pressed,
  And my door stood ready open for a long-expected guest,
But he never never came, night or morn.

Perhaps if I wait till the summer swallows flee,
  He will wander down the valley and meet me as before,
  Or perhaps he will find me alone upon the shore
When he comes with the swallows over sea.

AFTERNOON

DAPHNIS.

HERE, where the elm-tree shadows flicker thin,
Tall hawthorn hedges shut the meadow in;
And on this little slope beside the hedge
The grass leans softly to the water's edge.
Here let us sit and watch the sunlight fall,
And hear the stockdove to the stockdove call.

THYRSIS.

Down this hedge-path how many a time has gone,
Hand fast in hand, Phillis with Corydon.
In the deep stillness of this midland clime
Time passes leaving scarce a trace of time.
The silent-slipping seasons pass away;
Morning by evening day treads close on day;

AFTERNOON

The old harvests ripen, the new harvests grow
Now as they did a hundred years ago.

DAPHNIS.

Now as a hundred years ago the light
Lies golden on the gentle wooded height,
Where through the oaks and chestnuts glimmers red
The House of life beside its close of dead.
And there the meadow path runs half a mile
Below yon shadowing elms from stile to stile,
The stiles we lingered at, the path we know;
Ah me, that was not many years ago.

THYRSIS.

All that was over when the woods were wet:
Now the deep cornfields slumber and forget:
The heavy seeded rye-grass hangs asway,
The faint dog-roses tremble on the spray;
Poppies and great white daisies in the dew
Morning by morning are uncurled anew.
Now is the year's perfection; why should we
Put gladness by to live with memory?

DAPHNIS.

Thyrsis, the year's perfection is to me
Other than this; a hillside by the sea
Far south, and sheep-walks winding on the turf
Fragrant with close-cropt thyme; deep down the surf
Broke white unheard; beyond, right under us,
All the Atlantic lay monotonous,
One solid mass of blue in the August sun
That blazed above us.   But these days are done.

THYRSIS.

Night came, and morning comes after the night;
After the battle rest if not delight.
Rose ever morning fairer than that day
When slain and trampled in the mountain-way
The hope of the world lay breathless, and the air
Throbbed faint with heavy pulses of despair,
While riotously the flaring of the feast
Far on the plain outshone the whitening east?
Deep in the dawn a single star was pale,
Deep in the wood a single nightingale
Severed the darkness with sweet piercing pain;

And from the dewy dim Thessalian plain
A light wind rose, and like a hope, upborne
Tremulous and splendid from the gates of morn
Passed softly southward, gathering as it went,
Till all the golden wheatfields swayed and bent
Beneath its breath ; and with the widening dawn
Through dim ravines and gorges long-withdrawn,
Climbed to Parnassus' height, and carried down
Morning to the white temple and shining town,
And carrying morning with it, fluttered free,
And lightly ruffled up the sleeping sea;
Leaving behind it, faint and far-outspread
The mountain-pass with those three hundred dead
Stretched silent, and the morning mists unrolled,
And day returning with his shafts of gold.

DAPHNIS.

Day follows night, and night treads close on day,
And song and singer rise and fall away.
Might song and sunlight even on pain like mine
Descend for amulet and anodyne !
As if our madness thus might find relief,
Or Love could learn to melt at mortal grief!

THYRSIS.

Yet in this tranquil air and grassy place
Golden and gracious, why should pain have place?
Summer is not yet over; Love our lord
May yet descend upon our pastoral sward,
Light in his eyes as in this sunlit stream,
And all our sorrow vanish like a dream.

DAPHNIS.

So be it; but our afternoon is done;
The rooks stream homewards, and the sinking sun
Slants through the elm-branches that half the day
Have rustled faint above us.   Come away.

BALLADE

O Love, whom I have never seen,
   Yet ever hope to see;
The memory that might have been;
   The hope that yet may be;
The passion that persistently
   Makes all my pulses beat
With unassuaged desire that we
   Some day may come to meet:

This August night outspread serene,
   The scent of flower and tree,
The fall of water that unseen
   Moans on incessantly,
That line of fire, where breaks the sea
   In ripples at my feet;
What mean they all, if not that we
   Some day may come to meet?

BALLADE

About your window, bowered in green,
  The night wind wanders free,
While out into the night you lean,
  And dream, but not of me,
As now I dream of you, who flee
  Before my dream complete
The shadow of the day when we
  Some day may come to meet.

Envoy.

Princess, while yet on lawn and lea
  The harvest moon is sweet,
Ere August die, who knows but we
  Some day may come to meet?

TO COMATAS

—τὺ δ' ὑπὸ δρυσὶν ἢ ὑπὸ πεύκαις
ἁδὺ μελισδόμενος κατακέκλισο, θεῖε Κομᾶτα.

HERE on this garden's close-cut grass,
  Where here and there a leaf astray
Lies yellow, till the wind shall pass
  And take it some new earthy way,
Here, O Comatas, let us lie
While yet the autumn sun is high.

The stir of men is quiet now,
  But birds are singing each to each ;
The robin on the apple bough
  Sings to the robin in the beech,
And swallows twitter as they go
Wheeling and sweeping high and low.

No sound but these sweet madrigals
    To our enclosed garden comes,
Save when a ripened apple falls,
    Or gnats intone, or a wasp hums.
Here shall thy voice bid time speed by,
O boy Comatas, as we lie.

Sing some old rhyme of long ago,
    Of lady-love or wandering knight,
Of faithful friend and valorous foe
    And right not yet estranged from might.
The songs our singers sing us now,
O boy Comatas, sing not thou.

Sing, for thy voice has gentle power
    To cancel years of fret and woe,
And I remembering this one hour,
    Shall pass sad days the happier so.
And thou before the sun has set,
O boy Comatas, wilt forget.

RONDEAU

Most sweet of all the flowers memorial
    That autumn tends beneath his wasted trees,
    Where wearily the unremembering breeze
Whirls the brown leaves against the blackening wall;
More sweet than those that summer fed so tall
    And glad with soft wind blowing overseas;
    Through all incalculable distances
Of many shades that swerve and sands that crawl,
        Most sweet of all!

When comes the fulness of the time to me
    As yours is full to-day, O flower of mine?
Touched by her hand who evermore shall be
    While the slow planets circle for a sign,
Till periods flag and constellations fall,
        Most sweet of all.

*" Heere's a few Flowres, but 'bout midnight more:
The hearbes that haue on them cold dew o' th' night."*

Rose and lily, white and red,
From my garden garlanded,
These I brought and thought to grace
The perfection of thy face.

Other roses, pink and pale,
Lilies of another vale,
Thou hast bound around thy head,
In the garden of the dead.

NOCTURNE

CHOPIN, OP. 40, 2.

Is it so long, the sorrowful sad night?
But day will break, and bring the happy light,
   And then I shall arise and see the sun.
Nay, for the night has dawned eternally,
The shadow of death is heavy over me,
   There is no rising up for such an one.

No gay glad day, no quiet twilight hour,
No mist of morning or sweet noonday shower,
   No twitter of birds or murmur of labouring men ;
Only the wizard mockery of the moon,
The wind repeating the same weary tune,
   The dreams that light a little and fly again.

NOCTURNE

CHOPIN, OP. 37, I.

WHAT are ye looking for, ye poor eyes
   That turn so wearily to the night?
    O thou that leanest there from the sill
Of the room where the lamplight dims and dies,
   The stars are few and the moon is bright,
     And the trees in the street are asleep and still,—
   O wakeful dreamer, what dost thou see?
Only the wonder of earth and sky, and things too great for me.

What art thou looking for, thou poor heart
   . That beat'st thy wings like a prisoned bird?
    What bygone promise murmurs again
Of something secret and set apart
   That eye hath not seen nor ear hath heard
    To give thee solace of wrong and pain?

NOCTURNE

O heart, what vision hath come to thee?
Only the wonder of fond desire, and a hope too high for me.

(From the lighted church outside comes the sound of voices singing:)

    Life is short and time is flying,
    All our days are full of sighing;
    All our hopes are vain and lying—
        Power and riches, love and fame.
    One thing only faileth never,
    And for all our void endeavour,
    Still the cross must meet us ever,
        Still the sorrow and the shame.

    Is there any that complaineth,
    And a life of ills disdaineth?
    Naught but trouble still he gaineth,
        Seeking gifts of earthly store;
    In the heavenly kingdom rather
    All thy treasure strive to gather,
    Where Christ reigneth with the Father
        And the Spirit evermore.

What art thou looking for, thou poor soul?
  Canst thou recover that which is lost?
    O bruised and smitten, but not with rods,
Is there any hand that can make thee whole?
  O thou afflicted and tempest-tost,
    Thou suppliant, outcast of all the gods,—
  O soul, what remedy can there be?
Nay, there is naught but sorrow and fear, and a doubt
  too deep for me.

LOCA SENTA SITV

The rushes stand where the rushes stood,
   Stiff and tall, but the lake is dry;
They will stand so still in the lonely wood,
      Till the world shall die.

No wind makes rustle the weary reeds;
   The gentle gale and the rushing blast,
As they follow where spring or the storm-king leads,
      Pause aghast.

The red sun flames with a steady light,
   No smallest cloud in the brazen skies;
The moon looks down with a pale affright
      In her quiet eyes.

No song of bird can now come near,
No buzz of insect ever again,
No ripple of pleasant water, or tear
    Of the dripping rain.

The reeds stand now where the reeds then stood,
Above them hangs the silent sky;
Around them shivers the lonely wood,
    And the lake is dry.

A PASTORAL

" Tanquam nihil habentes, et omnia possidentes."
"Perchè pensa? pensando s'invecchia."

My love and I among the mountains strayed,
   When heaven and earth in summer heat were still,
Aware anon that at our feet were laid,
   Within a sunny hollow of the hill,
A long-haired shepherd lover and a maid.

They saw nor heard us, who a space above,
   With hands clasped close as hers were clasped in his,
Marked how the gentle golden sunlight strove
   To play about their leaf-crowned curls, and kiss
Their burnished slender limbs, half-bared to his love.

But grave or pensive seemed the boy to grow,
   For while upon the grass unfingered lay
The slim twin-pipes, he ever watched with slow
   Dream-laden looks the ridge that far away
Surmounts the sleeping midsummer with snow.

These things we saw; moreover we could hear
    The girl's soft voice of laughter, grown more bold
With the utter noonday silence, sweet and clear:
    " Why dost thou think ? By thinking one grows old.
Wouldst thou for all the world be old, my dear?"

Here my love turned to me, but her eyes told
    Her thought with smiles before she spoke a word ;
And being quick their meaning to behold
    I could not chuse but echo what we heard:
" Sweet heart, wouldst thou for all the world be old?"

LVNA FATIFERA

THE wind that had been blowing all the day
Seemed to have sobbed itself to sleep at last,
Like a tired child, and like a disc of gold
The sun slid down behind the furthest hill.
And then came voices in the silent air,
And voices in the tree-tops hushed and sad,
And then these died away; and as when men
Waiting to see a pageant hold their breath
And hear their heart beat, so the whole wide heaven
Seemed quiet with great longing for a space.
And then the wind began a low slow song,
And all the trees broke silence, and the birds
Roused from their slumber; and I looked and saw
The pallid circle of the risen moon
Betwixt the branches, but no stranger sight.
And still the wind sang louder as the moon
Wheeled higher and the trees threw deeper shade.
When the last red had vanished from the west
I wandered idly thro' the empty roads
Which seemed full of the stillness, past the fields

Where all day long the bending husbandmen
Had sheaved the corn, down the long village street,
And thro' the wicket where the hill descends
To find its grave in the encroaching sea.

    The sky was blue and cloudless, star by star
The innumerable company came forth
And seemed to watch and listen, and the moon
Shone white and splendid on the rippling sea.
I wandered down the hillside watching her
And heard the indistinguishable roar
Of ocean ever nearer, till at last
I stood upon the shingle; and the sea
Was maddened with the sadness of her eyes,
And cast itself in foam upon the beach.
And ever did it seem a messenger
Must come across the silver-paven sea
Out of the darkness round her to the shore.
But there came nothing save the wind that moaned
And the hoarse roll of breakers on the beach.
And then it seemed that I must go to her
Across the strait and climb the darkened stair.
But the great sea disdained a human tread,
And I could only wait and gaze and gaze
Till Sleep came unawares and sealed mine eyes.

OPISTHEN

Thy path is set through dust and mire,
   In waste lands dreary and forlorn,
   In lands where weeds outgrow the corn,
And nothing is that men desire.

The Hours, unseen, are at thy side
   With wings reluctant and with hands
   Outstretch'd to lead thee to the lands
Where all the year is summer-tide.

But backward thou dost turn to mark
   What lovelier form thine eyes may see
   In all the measureless to be
Emerging from the distant dark.

And while thou heedest not, their wings
   Are lightly spread, and they speed by;
   Nor will thy prayers and ceaseless cry
Recall them, nor thy sorrowings.

OPISTHEN

And others come as fair as they
   And others go, despised, unwoo'd;
   And thou in thy relentless mood
Art ever waiting by the way

Till she, thy love, at last appears;
   And in her eyes is no desire,
   Nor glow from out Love's altar-fire
But bitter vials of cold tears.

VIGILATE ITAQVE

The restless years that come and go,
The cruel years so swift and slow
Once in our lives perchance will shew
What they can give that we may know;

Too soon perchance, or else too late;
We may look back or we may wait;
The years are incompassionate,
And who shall touch the robe of fate?

Once only; haply if we keep
Watch with our lamps and do not sleep,
Our eyes shall, when the night is deep,
Behold the bridegroom's face,—and weep.

Alas! for better far it were
That Love were heedless of our prayer
Than that his glory he should bare
And shew himself to our despair.

VIGILATE ITAQVE

Better to wander till we die
And never come the dooranigh,
Than weeping sore without to lie
And get no answer to our cry.

O child, the night is cold and blind,
The way is rough with rain and wind,
Narrow and steep and hard to find;
But I have found thee—love, be kind.

SONG OF HYLAS

Which the Mysian youths sing in chorus, after their fashion, by the river Ascanius, where the boy Hylas was stolen away of the Nymphs, as the poets feign.

STROPHE.

THEBAN Hylas, child divine,
    Whither stray thy wandering feet,
    By the pools where Naiads meet,
        Where the Graces kiss the Hours,
Where the Loves for fetters twine
            Pale and purple flowers?

Hast thou, all unwitting, found,
    Like Narcissus, in a stream,
    Sweeter face than maiden's dream,
        Lovelier eyes than god Apollo's,
When he makes the harpstring sound,
            And sad Echo follows?

SONG OF HYLAS

Has some god in jealous mood
　Smitten thee, as the west wind
　Drove the discus swift and blind
　　Right against the blameless brow
Hyacinthine, from whose blood
　　　　Sprang the flower of woe?

Dost thou with Amaracus
　And with Amaranthus rest,
　In a garden by the west,
　　Where the beds of spices shed
Cinnamon and calamus,
　　　　For thy feet to tread?

Antistrophe.

No, thou sleepest in cool grot
　Deep beneath the water floods,
　In a grove of scentless buds,
　　Where the silver fishes leap,
Where thy lover is forgot
　　　　In a dreamless sleep.

SONG OF HYLAS

Naiads kiss thy mouth most sweet,
   And thy cheeks, like vermeil rose,
   In a summer garden close,
     Near the silver-shining lily,
Not so white as thy white feet
         Hanging languidly.

O'er thy face and gleaming limbs,
   Smooth as polish'd ivory,
   Vein'd with blue of the deep sky,—
     O'er thy lovely neck and hands
Calmly the dark water swims
         On to many lands.

Round thee, as alone thou liest,
   Gaze the sea nymphs in surprise,
   Softly touch thy closèd eyes,
     Wonder at thy yellow hair,
Call thee, but thou ne'er repliest,
         Hylas, ever fair.

SECVNDVM ALTITVDINEM CAELI A TERRA....

O love, O love, I cannot dare to love you,
    I will try not to love;
As soon might heaven's flowers, the stars above you,
    Fall from above,

And be transformèd to buds of mortal blossom,
    Stars which can fade and die,
For you to pluck and fill your hands and bosom
    As you passed by,

As soon I hope could night be turned to morning,
    And morning changed to night,
As your sweet soul be touched with aught but scorning
    At my soul's sight.

O pray to God (I think that God will hear you,
    If any God there be,)
That I bring never my dishonour near you
    For you to see.

O pray to God (if God is good he loves you),
    Pray to him earnestly,
If ever to aught of love my presence moves you,
    That I may die.

Child, I were more than glad to die to-morrow,
    Truly to die were gain,
If I could spare you thus one pulse of sorrow,
    One sigh of pain.

Love, if my soul cut off in grief and sinning,
    Could get your Paradise,
Think you salvation would be worth the winning,
    Or heaven a prize?

Lo, if in lifting up mine eyes distressed,
    This bliss I yet might win,
To see far off the gardens of the blessed,
    You crowned therein;

SECVNDVM ALTITVDINEM CAELI A TERRA

Lo! if mine ears all other comfort wanting,
    Deafened and drowned in hell,
Could catch one faintest echo of your chanting,
    Were it not well?

See you now: dreams and words! as weak and aimless
    As leaves whirled on a stream;
But my poor love that seeks but to be blameless,
    That is no dream.

THE HISTORY OF PHILIP THE DEACON

A Pageant played at Oxford on Corpus Christi Day.

¶ *Hic incipit de baptismatum doctrinâ et impositione manuum.*

SIMON MAGUS.

I AM Simon the Sorcerer,
For negremauncy without peer,
In any kingdom far or near,
   Babel, Archage, or Rome.
I summon by my potency
The spirits of men unborn that be,
Who all their learning shew to me;
   They cannot choose but come.

PHILIPPUS.

Omnis scientia a Deo est.
All wisdom that is godly blest
Is ghostly given, and the rest
   Is devil's work, I wis.

But be baptized, and even so
Thy curious cunning straight forego,
Thy spirit shall be white as snow
   Which now as crimson is.

Simon Magus.

I will assay it, sith that I
Would fain win immortality,
And live in heavenly bliss for aye,
   When dies my body here:
For doctors of a later day
Shew me in many a subtil way
The soul shall live, though some say nay;
   I charge them now appear.

¶ *Hic apparent doctores quidam capâ et caputio induti. Dum introeunt curia fidelium auditur cantans 'Sanctus, Sanctus, Sanctus Dominus Deus Omnipotens, qui erat et qui est et qui venturus est.'*

Doctor Physicus.

Can life then live when life is dead?
Poor fools, who ignorantly sing.
You are but you, flesh, bones and blood,
A beating heart, a thinking head.

If heart stop beating, little good
That day will be your shawm-playing.

Doctor Musicus.

Nay, but that day most good of all.
This world is but a shifting shade
Where nothing is, and all things seem;
But music is noümenal,
The allegory of a dream
Of that in heaven by angels played.

Doctor Nominalis.

Tush! our vile bodies may go rot.
Who cares?   Not I.   My works shall live.
My words shall sound for aye, although
My name, my memory be forgot.
My words, my works are I, I know
These only life eternal give.

Doctor Mathematicus.

We have but three dimensions;
Our shadows have but two, and they
Have other shadows with but one.
Thus suns are shades of other suns,

And thus on earth is heaven begun,
And Time is but Eternity.

Philippus.

I cannot this high sophistry
Right well devise; nathless I see
These clergy from a far country
   Have wisdom wonderous:
Now dip thee here, the whiles that I
Mark thee with cross *In nomine
Trino Patris et Filii*
   Et Sancti Spiritûs. Amē.

Petrus.

Here to Samaria am I led,
To these folk newly christenèd,
That Holy Spirit may be shed
   By blessing of my hands.

Simon Magus.

Give me this power, that on whomso
I lay my hands like grace may grow:

Lo, here is money, yea, and mo
   Shall be at thy commands.

Petrus.

For-fare thy gold and thee : God wot,
Herein thou hast no part nor lot,
Sith that for money thou hast thought
   To chaffer Holy Ghost.
Thou art in gall of bitterness
And veriest bond of wretchlessness.
Penance be thine and shrift endless,
   Or thou art merely lost.

Simon Magus.

Mahound hath me, withouten end,
Whom I had thought this tide to shend ;
Now am I his to rack and rend
   For that I God did jape ;
Lo ! I am damned, that is certain,
I may not be baptized again ;
Yet pray for me, good Christian,
   That I this woe may scape.

Angelus Domini.

Arise, and go toward the south,
Unto the land of sand and drouth;
The Lord God bids thee by my mouth.

Explicit Pars Prima.

Incipit Pars Secunda.

¶ *Via sit contra meridianū, quæ descendit ab Hierusalem in Gazam; hæc est deserta. Tunc intrabit vir Æthiops, sedens super currum legensque Esaiam profetam.*

Æthiops.

"He died in judgement and humiliation,
And now his life is taken from his nation,
And what man shall declare his generation?"

¶ *Hic audiatur vox Spiritûs Dei, qui pronunciet,*

Go near, and join thee to his chariot.

Philippus.

O prince, thou say'st hard sayings, yet God wot,
True sayings withal, if thou may'st understand.

Æthiops.

Nay, how? for I have prophet none at hand
Who may expound and tell me of whose death
The holy man of God prophesieth.

Philippus.

Hearkeneth now a mystery,
Which prophets old desired to see,
Yet did not see but fell on sleep.
And now the weakest eyes that weep
Have seen the vision, and the dumb
Proclaim the message—"Christ hath come!"
O king, thou knowest how a Jew
Not many Maundays gone they slew,
Because he said, "I am the Son
Of God, who will that every one
Forsake his sin and follow Me."
This, whom Esaias saith, is He.
Also thou know'st, what need to tell
How many a mighty miracle
He wrought upon the poor and sick;
Yea, and their dead He raised up quick;

And taught them a more perfect way
Of serving God. Howbeit they
Believed not, but some clave to Him.
Whom therefore in Jerusalem
They crucified, and in the grave
Laid Him, who came their souls to save.
But He arose on the third day;
And we are witnesses, who say
That He ascended into heaven;
And unto Him the world is given,
Which He shall judge at the last day.
And because men, being dust alway,
Can never grow like God unless
God clothe them with His righteousness,
He wills that they be born again
Like children without spot or stain.
And for our hearts are hard, and we
May not believe unless we see,
Lo, he hath left us for a sign
Of this new birth, water; and wine
And bread to make us grow in grace,
And fit to stand before his face.

Æthiops.

Lo here is water, see
What then doth hinder me
To be baptized by thee?

¶ *Hic exeant velut in aquas.*

Angelus Custos.

Bear thou the cross;
Earth's gain is loss,
Earth's wealth is dross,
   The Spirit saith.

Christ crucified,
And none beside,
Shall be thy guide
   While thou draw'st breath.

But persevere,
And bear it here;
Thou shalt not fear
   The second death.

¶ *Hic voces Cherubim audientur cantantium.*

Lo, from the midst God's holy habitation
    Through all the earth a living stream was sent;
A rushing mighty wind to every nation
    Who take God's ordinance and are content;
Water of death, fire of regeneration,
    To Jews offence, to Greeks astonishment.

ÆTHIOPS.

The priest is vanished as a dream of night.
What passionate ardour, what divine delight
Fills me and thrills me through with fire and light?
I did but dip myself but once, and lo!
Through all my veins I feel a new life grow.
I go my way rejoicing as I go.

PHILIPPUS.

I hear all round a noise of wind and fire
And distant thunders ever drawing nigher,
And distant voices of a heavenly quire.

   .   .   .   .   .

The sands are gone, the proselyte is gone
Whither I know not; in a land unknown
Mid a strange people I remain alone.

EXPLICIT.

ON A DRAWING OF LIONARDO IN THE ACADEMY AT VENICE

I.

O THOU that lookest forth with that strange smile
    Ever to thine and our great master dear,
Which, whether born of simpleness or guile,
    Still brings some sense of vague mistrust and fear,
    A smile which seems to fade as we draw near,
Tell us from what far country dost thou come,
For truly this our earth is not thy home?

II.

From what unknown far country not of earth
    What message dost thou bring us from the hand
Of him who, while he lived here, gave thee birth,
    Who now dwells ever in the charmèd land,
    Whence he could draw, like Prosper, with his wand,
Thee and thy brethren, an enchanted quire,
To grieve our hearts with unfulfill'd desire?

III.

O eyes divinely fresh in light of youth!
   O lovely childish head of doubtful sex!
O guide perplexing on the road of truth!—
   Then, is thy mission only to perplex?
   Surely thy maker made thee not to vex
Our souls?   No, in those tresses crowned and curled
He wove and set the riddle of the world.

IV.

O virginal soft mouth of girl or boy,
   Mysterious lips which praise not nor reprove,
Will you not say one word to bring us joy?
   Will you not speak, and tell us, "I am Love"?
   Thy sweet lips move not, though they seem to move.
And so perchance 'tis best, for, had they breath,
Who knows they might not answer, "I am Death"?

LINES BY A PERSON OF QUALITY

The loves that doubted, the loves that dissembled,
That still mistrusted themselves and trembled,
   That held back their hands and would not touch;
Who strained sad eyes to look more nearly,
And saw too curiously and clearly,
   What others blindly clutch;

To whom their passion seemed only seeming,
Who dozed and dreamed they were only dreaming,
   And fell in a dusk of dreams on sleep;
When dreams and darkness are rent asunder,
And morn makes mock of their doubts and wonder,
   What should they do but weep?

CONCERNING ACME AND SEPTIMIUS

(FROM CATULLUS.)

WHILE on his breast his Acme lay
"My darling," did Septimius say,
"If love can e'er more desperate be
Or fonder than my love for thee,
If lover e'er so loved before
As I will love thee evermore,
May I alone in Libyan land,
Alone on the parched Indian strand,
With none to help me, fall the prize
Of some great lion with great green eyes."
   Love heard, and now assured quite,
   Sneezed benediction on the right.
But Acme lightly bent her head,
And thus to her sweet boy she said,

Kissing with those red lips the eyes
Where love lay drunk in ecstasies:
"Ah, my dear life, so may we own
This our lord Love, our lord alone,
As melts my heart with fiercer glow
Than any passion thou canst know."
    Love heard, and now assured quite,
    Sneezed benediction on the right.
From this good omen now they start,
Love and are loved in heart and heart.
Lovesick Septimius loves one may
Than Britain more or Syria.
She faithful, all love's joy and boon
Finds in Septimius alone.
Say, when did Venus smile more fair?
Say, when were mortals happier?

FOR A DRAWING

(Ἐρᾶν ἀδυνάτων νόσος τῆς ψυχῆς.)

CLING closer, closer yet, love; so thy cheek
   Press mine and rest, and wreathen on thy head
      The jasmine plucked in the same sunny place
      Kiss and be once more mingled for a space
   With my faint myrtle,—once ere both be dead;
O close thine eyes awhile,—what do they seek?

O love, O love, content thee; cease from sighs
   Of which in the old days our lips were fain.
      What need for sadness now? All that is past.
      Or dost thou grieve because the hours fly fast?
   Beloved, shall not kisses stay the pain,
And ease the eternal hunger in thine eyes?

Smile, love, or I shall weep; say one word, sweet,
   And break the mournful spell ere the tears fall.
      What need for tears? What burden troubles thee
      From which an hour ago thy soul was free?
   O ask not more than life can give, for all
Thou canst desire is ready at thy feet.

Are things on earth no longer fair, love? Nay,
   Lift then thy drooping head to look around,
      Thy flower-crowned flower-like head, fairest of
         things
      Where all are fair; see how the summer brings
   Fresh light of flowers from out the kindling ground,
And buds blow now we knew not yesterday.

From the Italian of Giovanni Dell' Isola

Circ. A.D. 1485.

"There shall be no more sea," the seer saith,
Beyond the dark and silent strait of death,
   Purple like wine, or blue as summer skies,
Or fleecy white beneath the Nereids' breath.

Methinks the aged seer in some strange wise
Was rapt into Love's inmost Paradise,
   And saw the Apocalypse of heaven afar,
Gazing in Love's unfathomable eyes;

Eyes of fine fire that weeping cannot mar,
More clear and crystalline than any star.
   O Love, in heaven what need of any sea?
Thine eyes are deeper than the deep seas are.

Thy voice reverberates all the mystery
And music of all waters that can be:
   Voices like flutes blown soft in unison,
And thunders of tempestuous harmony.

O Love, what need have we of any sun
Or moon in thine own city, whereupon
   The light shed from thy bright hair's aureole
Makes pale the lustrous candles round thy throne,

O Love, with hair aflame and shining stole,
Who rose with wing'd feet from the flash and roll
   Of waters where yet all things were as one,
First of the Gods and Saviour of the soul?

MAGDALEN WALKS IN WINTER

A SHEET of water set about with trees,
  Bare branches black against the evening sky,
  And black reflected in the leaden mere ;
The chill forbidding waters seem to freeze,
  Save when an outcast wind unwillingly
    Shudders across their surface as in fear.

Out to the west the sky is dusky red,
  And cleft in sunder by that lovely tower
    Crowns its dim pinnacles with one dim star ;
Lo, for a signal that the day is dead
  The chapel bells toll out and tell the hour,
    Answered by city echoes from afar.

Winter is passing by us where we stand ;
  Can you not hear his footfall on the mould
    And catch his breathing through the twilight air ?
All things are dumb and patient to his hand,
  Whose guerdon is the darkness and the cold,
    The cold like death and darkness like despair.

SEPARATION

Quis dabit mihi pennas sicut columbae, et volabo, et requiescam.

Let us not strive, the world at least is wide;
This way and that our different paths divide,
Perhaps to meet upon the further side.

We must not strive; friends cannot change to foes;
O yes, we love; albeit winter snows
Cover the flowers, the flowers are there, God knows.

And yet I would it had been any one
Only not thou, O my companion,
My guide, mine own familiar friend, mine own!

LITANY

O MOTHER earth,
Is this a time to be gay?
Is this a time for song and lyre and velvet-green attire,
When on thy fair domain
The wide-destructive rain
Pours without let and stint and famine hovers nigher,
Never far away?
O mother earth,
Hear us, we pray,
In time of dearth.

O sun in heaven,
Where is thine ancient might,
Where is the heat that bade us rest, where is the light
that blest?
Surely thou art asleep,
Or thou wouldst hear us weep;

Or thou art on a journey beyond the leaden west;
        Without thy golden light,
        O sun in heaven,
        Day is as night
        And morn as even.

        O autumn wind,
        Blowing so fierce and free,
Blowing the rain clouds up the sky, and the pools of
        water dry,
        The fans fall no more
        Upon the granary floor,
For the scythe and sickle are red with rust, and the
        reapers sit and sigh,
        And the corn is sad to see.
        O autumn wind,
        We pray to thee,
        Blow warm and kind.

        O great God Pan,
        Who givest all good things,
Who fillest the spiky ear with grain and loadest the
        groaning wain,

Did not thine altars smoke
With the firstlings of the flock?
Is it for grievous sin that thou plaguest us with rain
In these our harvestings?
O great God Pan,
The whole earth rings
With the cry of man.

Aug., 1881.

TYRUS

O Tyrus, who art situate
   Within the entry of the seas,
I God who made thee wax so great,
   Princess among the provinces,
I God will lay thee desolate.

Thou sealest up the sum; in thee
   Have cunning builders perfected
Thy beauty; pilots of the sea
   From far talk of thy goodlihead;
Yea, ships of Tarshish sing of thee.

Fine linen out of Egypt is
   Thy covering; in thy walls are found
Blue clothes and wrought embroideries
   In chests of rich apparel, bound
With cords, among thy merchandise.

TYRUS

With coral, agate, calamus,
   And all chief spices, night and day
Thy dwelling was luxurious:
   All precious stones from Raämah,
Beryl and topaz, sardius,

Sapphire and diamond, glistering
   Lay in thy courts; thy merchant folk
Out of far Eastern lands did bring
   To thee, as each new morning broke,
Strange riches from their seafaring.

Thy shipboards were of mountain firs;
   Tall cedars fell for masts for thee
In Lebanon; thy mariners
   Sat on broad thwarts of ivory,
Wrought by Assyrian carpenters.

The traffickers of Syria
   Occupied alway in thy fairs
From Helbon, Minnith, Amana,
   With emeralds and broider'd wares;
Thy ships from far Ionia

Brought fair-hair'd slaves through mist and snow :
   Yea, Dan with Javan also went
Within thy markets to and fro ;
   Thy merchants were the excellent
Of all lands : I God set them so.

Yea, thou art the anointed one,
   The covering cherub : stones of fire
Were for thy treading ; yet shall none
   Find thee by searching, in the mire
And stones men spread their nets upon.

Shall not the isles shake at the dread
   And sound of slaughter midst of thee,
When the pit holds thee and thy dead
   In low waste places of the sea,
With cities not inhabited ?

In that day thou whose rumour ran
   Through all the corners of the sea,
Thou shalt be no God, but a man,
   In face of him who slayeth thee,
For all thy craft Sidonian.

ARTIFEX AD ARTEM

When Youth and Pleasure,
   Being strong, are fain
To pass all measure,
   To break all rein;
When the mænad Passion
   In Bacchic mirth
Would find or fashion
   A heaven on earth;

When the eyes are too weary
   Even to weep,
   The lips to wail;
When daylight is dreary
   Twixt death and sleep;
When love seems madness,
And thought is sadness,
   And desire doth fail;

Then calm me, raise me,
   To bear my part,
Who serve and praise thee,
   Spirit of Art.

SANTA CRUZ

Monday, 20th April, 1657.

I.

PRAISED be the Lord who hath done most marvellous things for us,
    Our help by night and day;
Who hath made straight paths for our feet on land, and wings for us
    Across the ocean way.
Who hath put to shame his enemies' wrath and curses,
    Avenged his people's moan;
Terrible in his judgments, infinite in his mercies,
    Most sure unto his own.

II.

All the long winter we were sailing, sailing,
    The Spanish coast in sight;

Our ships grown foul, food scarce and water failing,
    And never a chance to fight.
Safe behind Cadiz forts the Spaniards lying
    Kept close and let us be,
While day by day more of our men were dying
    For sickness of the sea.
But when the blowing of March gales abated,
    A galiot came with news,
The Plate fleet from Peru was come, and waited
    Harboured in Santa Cruz.
So Admiral Blake called all his ships together,
    And set his sails to go;
And in fighting order through the April weather
    We went to find the foe.

III.

Thus we sailed southward, over showery spaces
    Of wandering water driven;
The sunlight and the moonlight in our faces,
    The stars by hosts in heaven.
The helmsmen steered, and the wind and water
    bore us,
    Till on a Sunday night

Pale thro' the rose-girt west shone far before us
    The island peak in sight.
And the sun sank, and where the west was paling
    Day glimmered and was gone.
All night and into the morning, softly sailing,
    The English fleet ran on.

IV.

There lay the fleet we had waited for these bitter
    Long months of tossing brine;
Thro' the mist we saw their long brass cannon glitter,
    Their long blue pennants shine.
Twenty-two great warships, and behind we counted,
    Where the low sea-wall runs,
Fort after fort, and rows of earthworks, mounted
    With line on line of guns.
But for all the guns of the fleet and forts that fenced them,
    The tideway perilous,
Were not the stars in their courses sworn against them?
    Was not the Lord with us?
With us who had swept the seas of every stranger,
    Made every foe take flight;

Who for God and the Commonwealth never had
    shunned a danger,
  And never lost a fight?
Should it be to fail at last we had outwintered
    The blown Atlantic foam,
With timbers waterwarped and bullet-splintered,
    And sick crews far from home?
Behind us the wind rose and the mist was lifted;
    Slowly beneath its breath,
Thro' the tideway under the castle guns we drifted,
    Into the jaws of death.
The sea-breeze freshened and the fleet ran shoreward,
    And over us in the sky
The red cross of the Commonwealth streamed forward,
    The Lord of Hosts was nigh.

v.

The Lord who had been with us, and who still should
    be with us,
  To make our feet to stand;
Who had dealt for his mercies' sake most marvellously
    with us;
  Who held us in his hand,

A slaughter-weapon furbished for the slaughter,
    A sword made keen to slay,
To make the blood of his enemies run like water
    Along the waterway.

VI.

Then as the *Speaker* and the *Swiftsure* leading
    Ran in and went about,
From below the castle flag a flash came speeding,
    A puff of smoke slid out.
At once there leapt from all the encircling crescent
    Light redder than the sun's;
And the air throbbed and thundered with incessant
    Roar and recoil of guns.
From all their cannon and culverins came raining
    Their shot across our track;
From all our decks and portholes, steadily straining
    Our gunners answered back.
Hour upon hour the battle-smoke grew blinder,
    Heavier the battle-breath;
Before each ship hell shuddered, and behind her
    Opened the mouths of death.
The red blood lay on the decks in heavy splashes,
    Where, choked in smoke and flame,

We ran the guns out, firing at their flashes,
    That told us where to aim.
And above the roar of cannon, and the screaming
    Of great shot thro' the air,
The red cross of the Commonwealth kept streaming.
    The Lord of Hosts was there.

VII.

So the great sea-fight raged, till the firing slackened,
    The smoke-drift cleared away;
And left to sight where, smouldering hulks and blackened,
    The silenced galleons lay.
And every sail that from the Indies followed
    The Plate fleet as it came,
Under the gurgling water lay sea-swallowed,
    Or floated wrapt in flame.
We had made their impregnable harbour unavailing;
    We had fought at last and won;
By the grace of the Lord our weary winter sailing
    That April day was done.
Under the castle guns, that still, tho' slower,
    Kept firing on their foe,

In the evening land-breeze, as the sun drew lower,
    We set our sails to go.
Then the sun sank, and the starlight rose to cover us;
    Day glimmered and was gone.
And the red cross of the Commonwealth floated over us,
    The Lord of Hosts led on.

VIII.

Praised be the Lord who hath given both toil and
    playtime,
    Heart-grief and heart's-desire;
Leading us on, a pillar of cloud by daytime,
    By night a pillar of fire.
Who hath brought with an outstretched arm his chosen
    nation
    From darkness into light;
Who hath openly shown his judgment and salvation,
    Within the heathen's sight.
To the glory of him who hath made our name most
    glorious,
    Our heart and blood be given,
While the Commonwealth in England reigns victorious,
    The Lord of Hosts in Heaven.

DOGGEREL IN DELFT

τὸ γὰρ μιμεῖσθαι σύμφυτον τοῖς ἀνθρώποις ἐκ παίδων ἐστίν, καὶ τὸ χαίρειν τοῖς μιμήμασι πάντας.—ARIST. *Poet.* 1448, b. 5.

Βαιὰ μὲν ἀλλὰ ῥόδα.

I. *Life.*

WHITE rose and red
In one garden-bed.

Red rose and white
For my love's delight.

White and red rose,
Which is fairer, who knows?

II. *Death.*

WHITE rose and red,
One and both dead.

Red rose and white,
In my love's despite.

White and red rose,
Which is deader, who knows?

CHIMES

I.

GLITTER of gold and of ivory
As Love's wings draw nigh.

Golden blossoms in Love's hand
From a flowerful land.

Stained gold and shivered ivory
Where Love's feet have gone by.

Dead gold strewn over foot and hand
In the hollow land.

II.

Flowers are fallen and songs are ceased,
For the wind blows out of the east.

East wind chilly and grey
And a dead weight at my heart to-day.

Shall not the lark and the rose hold feast
When the wind goes out of the east?

East flush rose-red out of the grey
And daylight dawn in my heart that day.

HALF-WAY IN LOVE

You have come, then; how very clever!
    I thought you would scarcely try;
I was doubtful myself—however
    You have come, and so have I.

How cool it is here, and pretty!
    You are vexed; I'm afraid I'm late;
You've been waiting—O what a pity!
    And it's almost half-past eight.

So it is; I can hear it striking
    Out there in the grey church tower.
Why, I wonder at your liking
    To wait for me half an hour!

HALF-WAY IN LOVE

I am sorry; what have you been doing
    All the while down here by the pool?
Do you hear that wild-dove cooing?
    How nice it is here, and cool!

How that elder piles and masses
    Her great blooms snowy-sweet;
Do you see through the serried grasses
    The forget-me-nots at your feet?

And the fringe of flags that encloses
    The water; and how the place
Is alive with pink dog-roses
    Soft-coloured like your face!

You like them? shall I pick one
    For a badge and coin of June?
They are lovely, but they prick one
    And they always fade so soon.

Here's your rose. I think love like this is,
    That buds between two sighs,
And flowers between two kisses,
    And when it's gathered dies.

It were surely a grievous thing, love,
   That love should fade in one's sight;
It were better surely to fling love
   Off while its bloom is bright.

The frail life will not linger,
   Best throw the rose away,
Though the thorns having scratched one's finger
   Will hurt for half a day.

What! you'd rather keep it, and see it
   Fade and its petals fall?—
If you will, why Amen, so be it:
   You may be right after all.

TRICOLOR

BLUE her kirtle was, I ween
>> (*doce amie*)
Red and white her face was seen:

White as lily in a mere
>> (*flors de lis*)
Floating on the wan water:

Red as apples in a croft
>> (*el tans d'esté*)
Which her maiden plucketh oft:

Blue her eyes as blue steel bright
>> (*les eus vairets*)
They have made my red heart white.

TO M. A. C. G.

(LEAVING ENGLAND.)

O FOR the great good gift or the loan of a little
    leisure just to be lazy;
Just to be lazy at least in some more sane and
    sensible way;
O to be just set free for a short sweet space from the
    cracked and the crazy
    Cares and the tiresome trifles that weary and worry
    from day to day.
O to be out of the reach and the realm for a while
    of this dismal and dun light,
    Darkness rather I call it, which serves us sadly
    here for the sun;
Misty and muddy and fog-and-rain-ruled land, who
    knowest naught of the sunlight,
    Would I could once be well quit of thee, cut the
    whole business and run.

O for a week at the Lakes, or at Milan, or Rome, or
    Siena, or Florence,
  O to go anywhere with you away ; to Jericho, Joppa,
    Japan !
I'm longing for light and warmth, and lo ! it's pouring
    in chilly torrents,
  And you're going over the seas to Spain and I to
    my medical man !

MONOLOGUE D'OUTRE TOMBE

(PANTOUM.)

Morn and noon and night,
   Here I lie in the ground;
No faintest glimmer of light,
   No lightest whisper of sound.

Here I lie in the ground;
   The worms glide out and in;
No lightest whisper of sound,
   After a lifelong din.

The worms glide out and in;
   They are fruitful and multiply;
After a lifelong din,
   I watch them quietly.

MONOLOGUE

They are fruitful and multiply,
   My body dwindles the while ;
I watch them quietly ;
   I can scarce forbear a smile.

My body dwindles the while,
   I shall soon be a skeleton ;
I can scarce forbear a smile
   They have had such glorious fun.

I shall soon be a skeleton,
   The worms are wriggling away ;
They have had such glorious fun,
   They will fertilize my clay.

The worms are wriggling away,
   They are what I have been,
They will fertilize my clay,
   The grass will grow more green.

They are what I have been.
   I shall change, but what of that?
The grass will grow more green,
   The parson's sheep grow fat.

MONOLOGUE

I shall change, but what of that?
All flesh is grass, one says,
The parson's sheep grow fat,
   The parson grows in grace.

All flesh is grass, one says,
   Grass becomes flesh, one knows.
The parson grows in grace;
   I am the grace he grows.

Grass becomes flesh, one knows.
   He grows like a bull of Bashan.
I am the grace he grows;
   I startle his congregation.

He grows like a bull of Bashan,
   One day he'll be Bishop or Dean.
I startle his congregation;
   One day I shall preach to the Q—n.

One day he'll be Bishop or Dean,
   One of those science-haters.
One day I shall preach to the Q—n.
   To think of my going in gaiters!

MONOLOGUE

One of those science-haters,
   Blind as a mole or bat.
To think of my going in gaiters
   And wearing a shovel-hat!

Blind as a mole or bat,
   No faintest glimmer of light,
And wearing a shovel-hat
   Morn and noon and night.

TO THE NIGHTINGALE IN SEPTEMBER

(VILLANELLE.)

CHILD of the muses and the moon,
   O nightingale, return and sing,
Thy song is over all too soon.

Let not night's quire yield place to noon,
   To this red breast thy tawny wing,
Child of the muses and the moon.

Sing us once more the same sad tune
   Pandion heard when he was king,
Thy song is over all too soon.

Night after night thro' leafy June
   The stars were hush'd and listening,
Child of the muses and the moon.

Now new moons grow to plenilune
   And wane, but no new music bring,
Thy song is over all too soon.

Ah, thou art weary! well, sleep on,
   Sleep till the sun brings back the spring;
Thy song is over all too soon
Child of the muses and the moon.

THE LAST TENNIS-PARTY

October, 1382.

TO E. L. F.

It was a garden party drear,
I came from there to come to here.

Of women there I counted ten;
I and Lord Harold were the two men.

The rest were away to the smallest child
Where pheasants labour to grow more wild.

Lord Harold was a jocund knight,
Ever to jape was his delight;

He placed his thumb where my stout ribs be,
" Dost love to play tenpins?" quoth he.

I am a serious knight and grave,
I murmured simply, " Mary save ! "

We played at tennis with might and main,
And then at tennis we played again.

The fair dames came and the fair dames went,
But we knights played on without let or stint.

They brought to Lord Harold the claret cup,
He heaved a sigh and he drunk it up.

They brought me an ice, and a little spoon
Silvery-white like a full moon.

And we played till the robins went to bed,
And Lord Harold and I were well-nigh dead.

But ah, not yet was the ding of doom,—
We were ushered into the drawing-room.

I saw Lord Harold grow ghastly pale,
Like a wan moon in a green dale.

You have seen when a boy has hooked a flat
When a salmon-trout he was angling at;

You have seen his face where the pike lie low
Till he draws his snare, and then they go;—
I looked not otherwise than so.

Ten ladies sat on that polished floor;
There was no escape thro' the closed door.

I looked at Lord Harold, but not a note
Could win a way from his parched throat.

I spoke and my voice rang strange and hoarse,
I spoke again and it sounded worse.
I said, "Indeed;" then I said, "Of course."

Then I bethought me of tales to tell,
Which all allow I have told right well.

I told them tales I have told to few,
I told them tales that were old and true,
I told them tales that were good as new.

But no voice broke the silence round,
And I reeled full thrice and fell in a swound.

How long I lay on the Persian mat
I know not, but soon after that
I rose, and looked round for my hat.

BALLADE OF DEAD THINKERS

TO C. S. R.

Where's *Heraclitus* and his Flux
   Of Sense that never maketh stay?
Or *Thales*, with whom Water sucks
   Into itself both Clod and Clay?
Or He, who in an evil Day
   Νόμος and φύσις first employ'd,
And of the Sum of Things doth say
   They all are Atoms in the Void?

Where's grave *Parmenides?* Death plucks
   His Beard; and by the *Velian* Bay
Sleeps *Zeno;* *Plato's* Pen their Crux
   Of *One and Many* doth portray.
Empedocles too, wellaway,
   His taste for Climbing, unalloy'd
By Prudence, led him far astray:
   They all are Atoms in the Void.

Where's *Socrates* himself, who chucks
  Up *Physics*, makes of *Sophists* hay,
Into *Induction* briskly tucks,
  And *Definitions* frames alway?
The good *Athenians* him did slay,
  His *Dialectic* them annoy'd.
And his Disciples, where are they?
  They all are Atoms in the Void.

Envoy.

Prince, tho' with these old names and grey
  Our peace of mind be half destroy'd,
Take comfort; say they what they may,
  They all are Atoms in the Void.

SOME FLOWERS

TO E. L. F.

Poets sing you fancies
　About Love and Death,
　　Night and Day.
Do not give them pansies;
　" That's for thoughts," one saith :
　　Give them bay.

If the soldier's quarrel
　Be for right, not might,
　　God and King,
Let them bind the laurel
　Round his brows at night,
　　Glorying.

For the lover roses,
　Roses for his love,
　　Till they die;

When the churchyard closes
  O'er them, strew above
    Rosemary.

Let the lean æsthetic
  Round his garden bower
    Lilies twine ;
If he's energetic,
  Give him a sunflower
    Leonine.

For the parson rueful
  Herb of grace, not sense
    Here is rue ;
Let the sleepy pewful,
  With a difference,
    Wear it too.

RONDEL

She passed me by,
  And said no word,
  I should have heard
The slightest sigh.

Capriciously,
  No fault averred,
She passed me by,
  And said no word.

O Love on high,
  With pity stirred,
  Send thine own bird
To ask her why
She passed me by.

TRIOLET

Under the sun
   There's nothing new;
Poem or pun,
Under the sun,
Said Solomon,
   And he said true,
Under the sun
   There's nothing new.

SONNETS

K

"Tush, none but minstrels like of sonnetting."
Loues Labour's lost, iv. 3, 158.

THE LOST SELF

Supposing there had been two brothers, twin
   At birth, who grew like young plants in the sun
   To youth, but one died, and the other one
Living fell lower every day in sin,
Betraying his own heart, yet kept therein,
   When all things else were lost and he undone,
   Love of the dead strong and unstain'd alone;
Which thing avail'd of pitying gods to win
This boon, Æneas-like to pass the gate,
   Living, of Death, and in the fields of Hell
And groves to nether Juno consecrate,
To meet the luckless shade of the boy; but he
   Turn'd his pale face away in loathing,—well,
Even so it is with my old self and me.

PVLVIS ET VMBRA

From which gate came this dream, O Proserpine?
    Deep in the haunted autumn of a grove
    Whose golden leaves no breath had power to move,
Hollowed for adoration like a shrine,
Lit with her looks as with lamps crystalline,
    But bowered and screened from the sun's light above,
    Through dusk and silence I beheld my love,
And my mouth ached till it should call her mine,
For still her maiden mouth and eyes were kind,—
    But when I stirred there came an eddying gust,
    And all her raiment changed to leaves wind-blown,
And all her woven hair became as wind,
    And her white face and throat wind-driven dust,
    And I shrieked out, and woke, and was alone.

UNDER THE CANOPY

Yes, it is good for us that we are here.
   Scarlet, and blue, and purple in the sky,
   The covering of the holy sanctuary
By day obscured, at last by night shines clear.
Lo, yonder sinking sun is flaming there
   In evening sacrifice to God most high,
   And yonder moon is praying quietly,
And her one star holdeth his taper near.

Yes, good for us, albeit men may say
   Could we climb higher past the paths of men,
   Vague mists would show for all that fine linen,
And all that purple and scarlet turn to grey.
   It may be, yet for us they keep their hue,
   And if thou climb beyond, there is still the blue.

ITALIAM NON SPONTE SEQVOR

The Trojan, when he left the queen of Tyre,
   Far out at sea looked back, and saw a light
   On land, where all the city-walls were bright
With flames reflected from a fatal fire;
And knew it not for Dido's funeral pyre,
   Yet trembled and was troubled at the sight,
   The while to westward, like untimely night,
The great ill-ominous thunder-clouds drew nigher.

Even like Æneas in these days must we
   Steer a doomed course in heaviness of soul:
   Above our heads dark heavens that flash and roll,
Beneath, the hunger of the moaning sea;
   A love in ruin on the forsaken shore,
   And ah, what perilous promised land before?

LOVE UNRETURNED

My soul, where is the fruit of thy long pain
   To render to the husbandmen above?
   Thou hast been watered by my tears of love
For that pure spirit whose serene disdain
Pierced like a ploughshare thro' thee, leaving plain
   Forgotten depths wind-sown, whereout I strove
   Unceasingly to gather what might prove,
In time of harvest, tares instead of grain.

"Alas," my soul said, "had but Love passed by
   And cast into the furrows, as he went
      Sowing beside all waters, in the spring,
Methinks I had borne fruit abundantly
   For God to garner, as He sits intent
      Above the angels at their winnowing."

THINGS NEW AND OLD

I.

Yet turn and pause a little ere thou go.
  Have we then nothing thou wouldst take with thee
  For the new way whereon thy feet must be?
For Time is long, and Nature's hands are slow,
Being eternal; nor may they who sow
  Reap of the harvest of their hands, nor see
  ·The issues of the path that wearily
Winds by alternate drought and overflow.

These pastures were our fairest; these were they
  Whose lilied sward we once were wont to extol,
  But now the mountain summits are thy goal
And thou hast chosen a newer lordlier way;
  So be it: yet turn and pause, O daring soul,
And let our evening light thee to thy day.

II.

Thy day that cometh ; if that lurid light
   Spread on the mountains be indeed the day :
   If that precipitous unremitting way,
Lit of dull fires, and girt about with night
And desolation on thy left and right,
   Lead to some heavenly city far away
   Beyond the windswept summits bare and grey,
Under such clouds as blot the heavens from sight.

Ah, for thy rest what shining mansions wait
   Having foundations as our city hath?
   What prints foretrodden mark thy wearier path?
What other country lies behind the gate
   Where as thou enterest, blindly, not in wrath
'Slow-swung the irremeable hinges grate?

JEALOUSY

I sigh and fain would think that you are true,
   I look and fain would think you are not fair,
   And fain would I believe you have a care
For me or him or aught on earth save you
Yourself; wherefore though I should greatly rue
   Your sure denial of my utmost prayer,
   It seemeth yet that I could better bear
This than a fierce anxiety undue.

No, love; this eve I'd rather hear you say,
   "I love you best," and still be in your thrall,
Although you said the same to him to-day,
   Than know for truth you care for naught at all.
Strange poise of mind! to will to hang alway,
   Rather than by a motion risk a fall.

MADONNA INCOGNITA

Lady, whose name I know not, but whose face
   I know so well and knowing find so fair,—
   A pale young face crowned by pale drooping hair,
Like hers whose image Tuscan painters trace
Kneeling within some cloistered holy place
   Where snowy lilies spring in sacred air,
   Before whom even the Angel kneels to bear
Greeting of God and hail her full of grace;

Thy very look brings back lost Italy
   And days more bright than these with sun and art,
What shall be said of that same art and thee?
   Do Fra Filippo's virgins lend thee part
Of that faint grace, or rather shall I see
   More worth in them, remembering what thou art?

THE EMPTY PLACE

May Love new-found be what lost Love has been?
   New flowers will blossom where the old flowers are
      shed,
   Again the lark make music overhead,
And underfoot again the grass be green.
But thou, poor heart, through winter nights unseen
   Above Love's grave (who sleeps and is not dead)
   Weepest, and wilt not so be comforted,
Heart-broken; even as Mary Magdalene;

When in deep twilight ere the break of day
   She hasted through the quiet garden ground
      Bearing sweet spices to the tomb with her;
But seeing it empty, and the stone away,
   At her Lord's voice sobbed on and turned not
      round,
      Supposing him to be the gardener.

BEFORE PARTING

Thou knowest if I have loved thee: say no more;
   Forgive me if thou canst, and let me go.
   Why not?   God knows it were much better so.
I thank thy kindness that so long it bore
With me and with my love, a burden sore;
   Now let us go our ways; I hardly know
   If I am sad or glad, but time must shew.
Only let things be as they were before.

And now I have somewhat to ask of thee,
   Just one thing only; I would hear thee say
      Thou lovedst me once.   Ah, hast thou then
         forgot
The way?   Well, it is naught.   But now I see
   Thy loved lips soften to the lie; yet stay,
      For pity's sake and love's sake, say it not!

AFTER PARTING

Last night where that steep pathway skirts the wood
   Which in lost springs our footsteps used to know,
   Where ever in spring the earliest violets grow,
We parted with few words; silence seemed good
To end with.   While together yet we stood,
   Silent we watched the wrathful afterglow
   That brooded o'er the marshy lands below
And turned their standing waters into blood.

But thunder-murmurs vexing all the night
   Seemed like an angry message from the dead,
     A voice of wasted and dishonoured years,
   That moaned reproach above my stricken head,
And only ceased, as fearful of the light,
     When morn came chilled and tranquillised with
         tears..

MAGDALEN GARDENS AND MAGDALEN BRIDGE

I.

HERE in these walks where May brings June to birth
  Peace reigns and rest ; these leafy aisles are free
  From harm of axe and hammer—every tree
Dense-clad with summer, and shrill-tongued with mirth.
Spirit of beauty, very God on earth,
  Earth loves thee ever and is loved of thee ;
  Is it by man alone that thou must see
Wrong done thee, thankless change and waste and dearth ?

Nay, but thou lovedst us too, in days gone by ;
  Wilt thou not turn and visit us in pity,
    Here where thou once wast wont to show thy face
To those whose sons forget thee or deny,
  -Before they have destroyed thy holy city
    And quite laid waste what was thy dwelling-place ?

II.

O ye philanthropists of wills and powers
   Well-nigh divine, who would make all things new
   In earth as heaven, and almost do it too;
Ye men of progress, who would plant the bowers
Of Eden with your villas, and its flowers
   Uproot that you might run a tramway through,
   To serve mankind and swell your revenue:
Will you leave nothing good we may call ours?

O yes; we know your mission is to bless,
And we are sick with selfish fantasies,
   And *When men ask for bread we give a stone*,
   Only we have a scripture of our own
Which saith *Man shall not live by bread alone*,
Even in your fire-new howling wilderness.

SUMMER AND WINTER

A SHADOWED garden in the cool of the day
   Faint from June heat; the last birds on the wing
   Noiseless; and where the yellow evening
Melted to blue, the first faint stars astray.
Silent we sate, for silence seem'd to say
   One word; and quietly, like a hidden spring,
   Rippled the noise of garden-watering.
The bells of Oxford sounded far away.

Dead hour of that dead evening, once again
   In the scent of this faded wallflower
   Thou liv'st, and I sit silent there by her.
And therewith bitterly, thro' the wind and rain
   That vex to-day this wintry Northern sea,
   My heart cries out, O living love, to thee.

IRELAND

1881.

UNDER the cloud that always lowers the same,
   Or only darkens to a deadlier tone;
   Under the cloud of anguish, lit alone
By angry gleaming of nocturnal flame,
She stands, disconsolate to praise or blame,
   Circled with sorrow as with the sea, and blown
   By alien winds on waters not her own,
Ireland, the homeless sister of our shame.

Ah yet, beneath such darkness for a shroud
   Did not of old the circling sea retire,
When the Lord God led forth that murmuring crowd
   That blind rebellious people, His desire,
With an high hand under the fire and cloud,
   A cloud by day, by night a pillar of fire?

IRELAND

1882.

Mother, awake! are night's encircling bands
   So heavy around thee, or so slow to fly
   The setting stars that singly pass thee by?
Carest thou not that here thy sister stands
Tearless and hopeless, mournfullest of lands,
   In rain and tempest holding wretchedly
   Against the iron blackness of the sky
Uplifted fettered weak indignant hands?

O nation not desired! blind is thy night
   And blind her sleep who will not wake nor turn,
   Yet even in slumber shudders to discern
In the dark west a glimmering menace of light
   Thro' clouds dim-canopied and deep-withdrawn,
   Pale on pale faces. Ah, is this the dawn?

ON THE BIRTH OF VENUS BY BOTTICELLI

Is it not strange, the difference there may be
   Between two works whose subject still is one?
   I saw, where Byron's goddess "loves in stone,"
Another Venus risen from the sea.
Watch that Greek godhead : can this, too, be she
   Wistful and pale by these young Zephyrs blown
   O'er waves to shore?   Can these pink roses strown
Be blossoms of that same divinity?

The same, yet not the same : to this new birth
   The world hath travailed for a thousand years,
And a changed Venus dawns on a changed earth
   From out a sea whose waves are salt with tears ;
And this our Love, since Greece lives not again,
If she give every joy gives too all pain.

ON A DRAWING BY BURNE JONES

I saw how Love was leading on a way
   Beset with stones and thorns that grew thereby
   A weary wight that seemed like to die
For all the wandering of that tedious day,
But Love upheld him so that he might stay;
   About whose wings myriad small birds did fly,
   That ever bear their Master company
And by their singing charm distrust away.

And as I pondered on this pitiful fate,
   Love spake: " The end of striving is not strife,
     The trees are bare that summer quickeneth;
And whoso entereth at Love's wicket-gate
   Shall find the way to everlasting life
     Lies through the valley of the shadow of death."

VENVS MATVTINA

She lies at dawn upon the dew-drenched lea
   Alone. The white hard light of morning lies
   On the throat wavering with the fall and rise
Of her low pulse as of a silent sea.
The thick coils of her hair cling shudderingly
   To her white shoulder; her deep-lidded eyes
   Heavily raised as in a dull surprise
Look through the vacant shadows vacantly.

Her back is to the sunrise; the low sound
   Of a stream slipping past incessantly
     Stirs in her raiment light and white as foam.
But she, her head erect, her hair uncrowned,
   With lax white feet and wrist dropped wearily,
     Gazes through heaven and earth and finds no home.

THE HANDMAID OF THE LORD

Look down a moment ; let thy lips uncurl
   Into some word for us too ; droop thine eye
   Once from the heavenly city, distantly
Seen with its twelve gates, each a several pearl,
Whereunder undistinguishably whirl
   Influent and refluent eternally
   The silent-streaming worlds; are these so nigh,
And we so far beyond thy seeing, girl?

Nay, for the evidence of things not seen,
   The substance of things hoped for, this we know ;
   But what is that whereon thou gazest so ?
   What splendours of the morning from above,
What glory of God is on thee?
                          "I have been
There, and seen Him who is the light thereof."

ON A MADONNA AND CHILD OF BELLINI

Years pass and change; mother and child remain.
   Mother so proudly sad, so sadly wise,
   With perfect face and wonderful calm eyes,
Full of a mute expectancy of pain:
Child of whose love the mother seems so fain,
   Looking far off, as if in other skies
   He saw the hill of crucifixion rise,
And knew the horror, and would not refrain.

Yet all that pain is over in very deed,
   And only love shines from those eyes alway;
Love to fulfil the world's enormous need,
   Light to illuminate the devious way,
Still brighter as the centuries recede,
   And more and more unto the perfect day.

THE NATURE OF THINGS

Sit hoc profecto certum, quoniam
    Humana cuncta parent huicce legi,
    Non posse dici, "hoc vel hoc peregi,
Et illud cras perinde peragam."
Dies arridet nunc, at ecce jam
    Nubes obtraxit imbrem ; neque venti
    Sic plena luna perflant ut crescenti,
Sed vertunt ac revertunt perperam.

Rerum natura nempe nil fatetur
    Tam gratiosum esse nec praeclarum
Quin obsolescat et obliteretur
    Quum tempus illud venerit amarum,
In quo de nocte nox continuetur
    Et illucescat instar tenebrarum.

TRANSLATIONS FROM THE GREEK

"Rose leaves, when the rose is dead."

FROM MELEAGER

I.

The windy winter from the sky is gone,
  The purple springtime brings the flowers with glee,
The wan earth puts her grassy garland on,
  And fresh leaves deck each quick'ning plant and
    tree.
Fed by soft dewdrops of the genial dawn,
  With opening roses all the meadows smile;
Clear pipes the shepherd on the mountain-lawn,
  And grey-haired kids the goat-herd's heart beguile.
Now o'er the sea's broad back the sailors fare,
  Unwearied Zephyr fills the swelling sail;
Now, wreaths of clustering ivy in their hair,
  To the grape-giver Bacchants shout all hail;
New-born from out the teeming heifer's womb
  The hivèd bees their curious labour ply,

And in the fretted hollows of the comb,
    The white fresh-flowing honeydrops lay by.
Now every tribe of birds sings clear and shrill,
    The twitt'ring household swallow in the dale,
The halcyon and the swan on wave and rill,
    And shadow'd in the grove the nightingale.
If then the forest boughs and leaves rejoice,
    If earth has burgeon'd and the shepherd sings,
And fleecy flocks make merry with one voice,
    And sailors go on their sea-wanderings,
When Dionysus leads his jocund quire,
    And winged songsters tune their various lay,
And bees go labouring on and never tire,
    Why shall the singer only not be gay?

FROM MELEAGER

II.

I WILL twine the violet,
And with soft narcissus set
Laughing lilies, and with these
Myrtles and sweet crocuses,
Hyacinth that purple blows,
And the lover-loving rose.
These for garland will I pour
On thy head, my Heliodore,
On thy locks of curling hair,
On thy tresses sweet with myrrh.

FROM MELEAGER

III.

Now white violets blow, and blows
The narcissus in the showers,
And the mountain-wandering
Lily, and at last the rose
Loving lovers, even she,
Peitho's child, Zenophile,
Flower of spring and flower of flowers,
Buddeth, sweetly blossoming.
Meadows, tho' your flowers are bright,
Tho' you laugh, your laugh is light,
For the maid is rarer far
Than your sweetest garlands are.

IV.

Bridegroom none but death alone
Has my Clearista won,
So to loose her virgin zone.

Yester eve the flutes blew sweet,
Bridegroom and the bride to greet,
And the bridal doors were beat.

Now at dawn they sound again,
But another sadder strain,
Hymen's song is hushed in pain;

And the torch that flared so gay,
Lighting up her bride's array,
Lit the dead her downward way.

FROM MELEAGER

V.

PHOSPHOR, farewell, thou herald of the dawn,
    And, swiftly gone,
As Hesper come, and bring back her, I pray,
    Thou steal'st away.

FROM MELEAGER

VI.

O POUR the wine, and as you pour,
Say *Heliodore, Heliodore,*
Ever and ever, o'er and o'er.

And bring a chaplet for my hair,
Yesterday's chaplet, sweet with myrrh,
To wear in memory of her.

Ah, look, the lover's rose distrest,
Is weeping now to see her rest
Otherwhere, not upon my breast.

VII.

Tears, bitter tears, all I can give,
   Tears to the depths, to thee I pour,
   To thee in Hades, Heliodore,
All of my love that there may live.

Tears, bitter tears, I pour to thee,
   Tears of libation, wept above
   Thy tomb, in memory of my love,
In memory of thy love to me.

Ah, with what sighs, with what tears shed,
   I, Meleager, mourn thy face,
   To Acheron a bootless grace,
To me still dear among the dead.

Alas, my blossom, whither must
   I seek thee now? Hades it is,
   Hades hath snatched away my bliss,
And trod the perfect flower to dust.

Yet shall not tears disturb thy rest.
   Rather, I pray thee, mother earth,
   Our mother thou, who gav'st us birth,
To fold her gently to thy breast.

VIII.

Love I cry, the truant love.
  Now, but now at break of day,
Did he from his couch remove,
  Spread his wings and fly away.

Ever-prattling is the child,
  Sweetly-tearful, laughing-sly,
Quiver-girt, of spirit wild,
  Swift of foot and swift to fly.

Who his father none can tell,
  Heaven and earth profess to me
They are not responsible
  For this brave; so says the sea.

All men hate him everywhere.
  Look you well in every part,
Lest unseen he lay a snare,
  Gentle hearer, for your heart.

Ah, the archer! there he lies,
  Hid beneath my mistress' brow,
In the shadow of her eyes,
  Darting at me even now.

FROM MELEAGER

IX.

Drink deep, wan lover, ay, drink deep,
In Bromius' gift thy senses steep,
And lull thy hopeless flame to sleep.

Drink deep, a full deep butt of wine,
And let the heart's true anodyne
Thrust forth this hateful love of thine.

X.

Sweet on the pipe, by Pan of Arcady,
    Sweet is thy song, and on the viol sweet.
I cannot fly, for Loves encompass me,
    And leave no breathing-space, no not one whit,
Or song or grace or beauty breathe desire
Or all at once, so I am all on fire.

FROM SAPPHO

When thou fallest in death, dead thou shalt lie, nor shall thy memory
Henceforth ever again ever be heard then or in days to be,
Since no flowers upon earth ever were thine, plucked from Pieria's spring,
Unknown also mid hell's shadowy throng thou shalt go wandering.

FROM ALCMAN

Maidens with voices like honey for sweetness that breathe desire,
Would that I were a sea-bird with limbs that could never tire,
Over the foam-flowers flying with halcyons ever on wing,
Keeping a careless heart, a sea-blue bird of the spring.

FROM CALLIMACHUS

O IF swift ships had never, had never sailed the sea,
Poor child of Diocleides, we had not wept for thee;
But now thy body is drifting on some unknown abyss,
And this thy name and empty tomb is all of Sopolis.

FROM MENANDER

TO B. N.

Him I call happiest, Parmeno,
Who having seen this solemn show,
The common sun, the clouds, the sea,
The stars and fire, not painfully,
Goes quickly back from whence he came.
For you would see them still the same
If you abode for two or three
Short years, or for a century;
But grander sights you would not see.

FROM LEONIDAS

TO A. H. B.

Now is the time to sail, for home
The twittering swallow now has come,
And Zephyr bloweth graciously.
Yea, and the meads are fair to see,
With spring-flowers, and the ocean still,
Where late the fierce winds worked their will,
And the wild wind went winnowing.
Heave up the anchor.   Shoreward fling
The hawser, pilot, and make sail
With canvas spread for every gale.
'Tis I Priapus bid thee this,
O man, whose charge the harbour is,
So may'st thou sail to every sea,
And bring thy merchandise with thee.

FROM THEOCRITUS

I.

Have a care of life, O man,
Seeing how small is all its span.
   In the season of fierce weather,
Put not out to sea,
Lest thou perish as did he,
   Ship and man together.
For he hasted without care
To bring home his Syrian ware,
Home to Thasos beautiful—
Cleonicus miserable!
When the Pleiades gan sink
   He put forth on stormy seas,
But never reached the further brink,
   Sinking with the Pleiades.

II.

WHITE Daphnis, he who pipes so clear
The songs our shepherds love to hear,
Offers to Pan these little wares,
Pierced reeds, a stick to throw at hares,
Sharp hunting spear and brown fawnskin,
And scrip he carried apples in.

A VINTAGE SONG

From Agathias.

As we trod thy wine-press, Iacchus, the bountiful infinite wonder,
 Weaving a song to chime with the rhythmic fall of our feet,
Flowed the ineffable stream as a swoln wave flowing thereunder,
 Danced our ivy-wood goblets like boats on the surges sweet.
And we said no Naiad should break the bond of our chorus asunder,
 As we drew from the vat and drank and were filled with the Bacchic heat.

But sudden over the must there lightened a splendour of roses,
 Rosier-red than the wine was the maiden bending above,

And our hearts bound fast in the net where Bacchus his lovers encloses,
Were bound more fast than before in the pitiless fetters of love.
Ah! but there at our feet the abundant river reposes,
And vain desire is all that the rose's lover can prove.

THE SWALLOW SONG

Sung by Greek boys from door to door when the first swallow came oversea.

Come, come is the swallow,
With fair spring to follow.
She and the fair weather
Are come along together.
White is her breast,
And black all the rest.

Roll us a cake
Out of the door
From your rich store
For the swallows' sake,—
And wine in a flasket
And cheese in a basket
And wheat-bread and rye,
These the swallow will not put by.

THE SWALLOW SONG

Will you give us or shall we go?
If you will, why rest you so;
But an if you shall say us nay
Then we will carry the door away,
Or the lintel above it, or easiest of all
Your wife within, for she is but small.
Give us our need
And take God speed.
Open door to the swallow then,
For we are children and not old men.

FROM SOPHOCLES

I.

My fortune circles ever in the pace
   Of God's revolving wheel,
And all its nature changes with its place.

Like as for no two nights the moon's wan face
   Can keep the same form still;
But first from out the unseen to birth is brought,
   Then grows in grace and night by night enspheres,
   Till when the fulness of her prime appears,
She dwindles back and comes again to naught.

II.

Like as in winter when the frosts appear,
    The children love to play amid the snow,
And in their little fingers without fear
    They take the ice that was the water's flow,
    And feel a keen delight they did not know;
But soon the crystal ginneth them to smart,
    And they ne wis to hold it ne forego.
So oftentimes a gentle lover's heart
Is lief to ease his woe, yet loth with bliss to part.

FROM THE ILIAD

The Greek and Trojan armies join battle.

As when sea-waves upon a sounding shore
Rise wave on wave, the west wind blows them up,
First out at sea a crest, and at the end
A breaker loudly bellowing on the beach,
And round the capes a crescent mounting high
Spitting sea-froth; so ever wave on wave
The Danaan army moved along to war.
Each chief called to his men; and they moved on,
A great crowd following dumbly. You would say
In all their hearts there was no human voice.
Silent they watched the signals, and on all
Shone dazzling armour, as they moved in rank.
  But as when sheep stand in some rich man's fold
Ten thousand, and white milk is drawn from them,
They bleat the while, hearing the bleating lambs,
So of the Trojans thro' the broad array
A tumult rose, for not to all alike
Was one same speech or voice, but mixed their tongue
Summoned from many lands; these Ares roused,

Grey-eyed Athene those, and Dread and Fear
And Discord sister of Ares, slayer of men,
Restless and eager, ever by his side.
Small is her stature first, but at the end
Her feet move on the earth, her head strikes heaven.
She moved then down the midst, and thro' the host
Cast mutual hate, and increase of men's groans.
   So when they came together to one place,
Shield clashed on shield, and spears and strength of men
In brazen armour clanged, and bossy shields
Closed on each other, and there rose a roar,
And with it cries and prayers of those who slew
And those they slew, and the earth ran with blood.
And as when winter torrents down the hills
Rush from their mighty founts where two glens meet,
And the strong streams meet in the deep ravine,
And shepherds hear the thunder on the hills,
Such was the roar and stress of meeting men.

www.ingramcontent.com/pod-product-compliance
Lightning Source LLC
Chambersburg PA
CBHW020846160426

43192CB00007B/809